First Facts®

Inspired by Nature

SAFETY INVENTIONS
Inspired by Nature

by Lisa J. Amstutz

raintree
a Capstone company — publishers for children

Raintree is an imprint of Capstone Global Library Limited, a company incorporated in England and Wales having its registered office at 264 Banbury Road, Oxford, OX2 7DY – Registered company number: 6695582

www.raintree.co.uk
myorders@raintree.co.uk

Edited by Abby Colich and Jaclyn Jaycox
Designed by Juliette Peters
Picture research by Jo Miller
Production by Katy LaVigne
Printed and bound in India

978 1 4747 8560 0 (hardback)
978 1 4747 8578 5 (paperback)

British Library Cataloguing in Publication Data
A full catalogue record for this book is available from the British Library.

Acknowledgements
b=bottom, l=left, m=middle, r=right, t=top
Alamy: Tribune Content Agency LLC, 17b; AP Images: Keith Srakocic, Cover, 7r; Newscom: Gus Regalado/Album, 21t; Science Source: Claus Lunau, 11t, Pascal Goetgheluck, 13br, Raul Gonzalez, 13bl, USDA/Peggy Greb, 5; Shutterstock: BalkansCat, 1l, 9, Christian Vinces, 11b, hxdbzxy, 7l, Kenny CMK, 19t, metamorworks, 15b, NaniP, 1m, 15t, Rawpixel.com, 19b, sahua d, 21b, Sten Roosvald, 1r, 17t, Yann hubert, 13t
Design Elements: Shutterstock: Zubada
Every effort has been made to contact copyright holders of material reproduced in this book. Any omissions will be rectified in subsequent printings if notice is given to the publisher.

Contents

Ideas from nature

Nature is full of good ideas. Some scientists study nature. They use what they learn to make new things. Copying ideas from nature is called biomimicry. Ideas from nature can help keep people safe.

Fact

The word "biomimicry" comes from the Greek language. "Bios" means life. "Mimesis" means to copy.

Scientists study nature to help solve human problems.

Search like a snake

Earthquakes and tornadoes damage buildings. People can become trapped inside. Rescue workers must find them quickly. It's a dangerous job. A "snake" robot can help. It moves like a real snake. It can squirm through **rubble**. Lights and cameras on the robot help the rescue workers to see inside.

Fact

Scientists are copying a snake's skin too. They studied how a snake can slither easily over objects. Some machines may one day move more like snakes.

---

rubble broken bricks, concrete, glass, metal and other debris left from a building that has fallen down

Watch your head!

A woodpecker pounds its beak on wood all day. But it doesn't hurt its head. Soft **cartilage** keeps its brain safe. One inventor used this idea. He made a safer bike helmet. It has special cardboard inside. It protects the rider's head.

cartilage strong, rubbery tissue that connects bones in people and animals

inspire to influence and encourage someone to do something

Fact

Other animals have also **inspired** new helmets. Scientists have made helmets using ideas from a turtle's shell and a hedgehog's spines.

Catching the waves

Dolphins use sound waves to find food. These sound waves move easily through water. Scientists have made **sensors** that can find sound waves underwater. They can pick up the sound waves from underwater earthquakes. Scientists use these sound waves to study **tsunamis**. Soon they may be able to warn people when a tsunami is near.

echolocation process of using sounds and echoes to locate objects; whales and dolphins use echolocation to find food

sensor instrument that detects changes and sends information to a controlling device

tsunami series of ocean waves caused by an underwater earthquake or volcano

Fact

The process that dolphins use to find food is called **echolocation**. Whales and bats use echolocation too.

Dolphins send out sound waves to find prey. The waves bounce off the prey and back to the dolphin.

Ants to the rescue

When ants face danger, they send out a signal. More ants come to help. They attack as a **swarm**. Computer scientists have used this idea. They made digital "ants". This "swarm" moves through a computer. The ants look for malware. Malware programs steal information and harm computers. Digital ants protect computers and keep information safe.

swarm large number of bugs together in a group

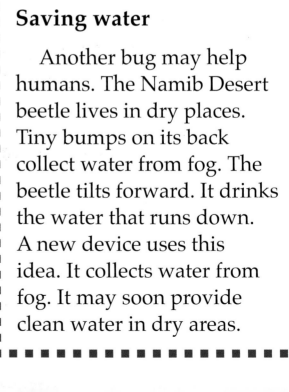

Saving water

Another bug may help humans. The Namib Desert beetle lives in dry places. Tiny bumps on its back collect water from fog. The beetle tilts forward. It drinks the water that runs down. A new device uses this idea. It collects water from fog. It may soon provide clean water in dry areas.

swarm of ants

MALWARE ALERT

SCAN NOW

Click here for more information

Fighting germs

A shark's skin is made of tiny toothlike plates. These plates help to stop **algae** and **fungi** from growing on the skin. Scientists have made a material that is like shark skin. It is used on hospital equipment. It stops germs from growing there. This material helps protect people from disease.

algae plant-like organisms that live mostly in water

fungi organisms that have no leaves, flowers or roots

resistant able to fight off or withstand something

Fact

Over time, some germs can become **resistant** to drugs. They can cause diseases that are difficult to treat. Shark skin material can help to stop these germs from spreading.

shark scales

shark skin material

15

A bug's eye view

Locusts fly in large swarms. But they rarely bump into each other. They focus on the insects right in front of them. Scientists used this idea. They are working on making sensors for self-driving cars. The sensors will detect objects around them. They will help to stop the cars from crashing.

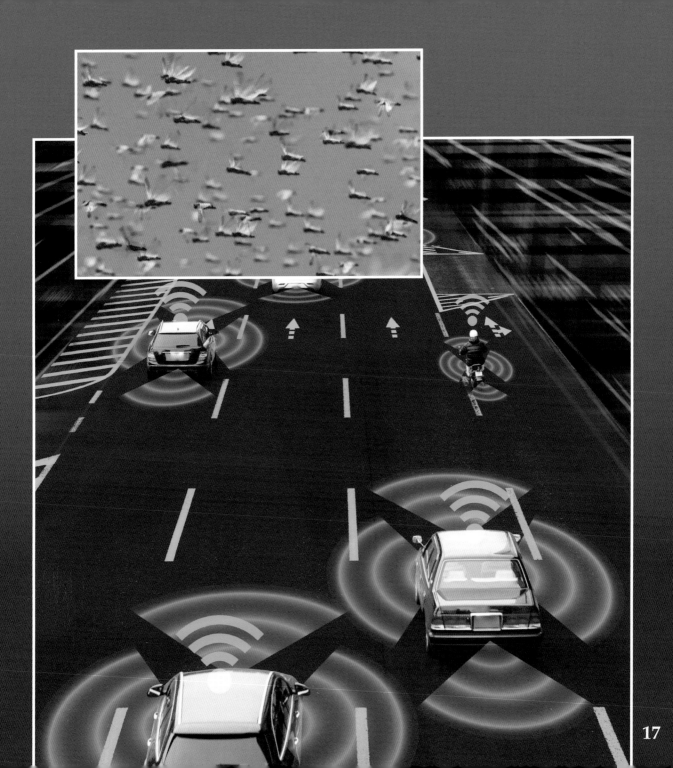

Spider's web glass

Thump! Birds crash into windows every day. But thanks to spiders, birds may be safer! Spiders' webs reflect **ultraviolet (UV) light**. Birds can see this reflection. Scientists have created a new type of glass. It reflects UV light in the same way that spiders' webs do. To people, the glass looks clear. But birds know to stay away from it.

---

ultraviolet light rays of light that cannot be seen by the human eye

Fact
Humans cannot see UV light, but many animals can.

From bats to scanners

Bats fly and hunt in the dark at night. They send out sound waves. They listen for the echoes that bounce back. The echoes help them find food. Airport scanners use the same idea. They send out sound waves. The echoes form an image on a screen. They help workers spot weapons inside people's clothes or bags. They help to keep travellers safe.

---

toxin poisonous substance made by a living thing

Turkey detectors

Bats aren't the only winged animals inspiring safety. The skin on a turkey's head changes colour with its mood. Scientists have studied how the skin does this. They have made an air sensor that works in the same way. It can find **toxins** in the air.

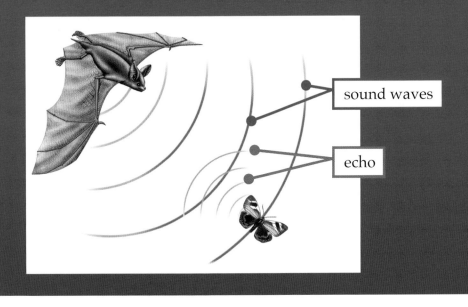

sound waves

echo

FULL-BODY SCANNER

② The body is scanned.

PLEASE
raise your arms
according to picture.

① Person is asked to raise his or her arms.

③ A scanned image appears on a computer screen.

Glossary

algae plantlike organisms that live mostly in water

cartilage strong, rubbery tissue that connects bones in people and animals

echolocation process of using sounds and echoes to locate objects; whales and dolphins use echolocation to find food

fungi organisms that have no leaves, flowers or roots

inspire to influence and encourage someone to do something

resistant able to fight off or withstand something

rubble broken bricks, concrete, glass, metal and other debris left from a building that has fallen down

sensor instrument that detects changes and sends information to a controlling device

swarm large number of bugs together in a group

toxin poisonous substance made by a living thing

tsunami series of ocean waves caused by an underwater earthquake or volcano

ultraviolet light rays of light that cannot be seen by the human eye

Find out more

Cat's Eyes to Reflectors (Tech from Nature), Jennifer Colby (Cherry Lake, 2019)

Everyday Inventions Inspired by Nature (Technology Inspired by Nature), Samantha Bell (Focus Readers, 2018)

Search-and-Rescue Robots. (Robot Innovations), Brett Martin (Abdo, 2018)

Websites

Everyday mysteries: biomimicry for kids
www.loc.gov/rr/scitech/mysteries/biomimicry.html

How we make stuff
www.made2bmadeagain.org/creatures_cwdtd

Learn about how to plan and design with BBC Bitesize
www.bbc.co.uk/bitesize/subjects/zyr9wmn

Comprehension questions

1. How does a "snake" robot help rescue workers?

2. Echolocation has inspired scientists to make underwater sensors. What is echolocation?

3. Can you think of another use for the shark skin material discussed on page 14? Explain why you think it would be helpful.

Index